THE
RIGHT
BUSINESS

A guide for business owners and teams who want to create, grow and
enjoy a successful and balanced business in their lives

ISBN: 978-1-5272-8194-3

CONTENTS

What is the right business for me?

I have often been asked by business owners to support them to create an ideal business for themselves, so that they can get the outcomes they want and enjoy the business they love.

The discussion often starts with the word **right**:

What is right for me?

What is right for my business?

What is the right thing to do in my business?

The right business is what is right for you.

There are three basic components:

The right business must have the Right Culture, with the Right Revenue, in a Functional Operation.

INTRODUCTION

Why write a book about business when there are already so many available?

The truth is, I did not intend to write a book on business. This book is about sharing many of my experiences acquired when coaching business professionals and their teams. You may wish to learn from these experiences, where it is applicable to you and your business.

Prior to working as a business and executive coach for the past 15 years, I trained as an architect; I managed and jointly owned an architectural practice in Scotland and grew the business to be one of the most successful architect businesses in the UK.

For family reasons, I exited from my business and was introduced to Shirlaws, an international coaching business, where I was trained and worked for 10 years across the UK, before I left and started my own coaching business in Scotland.

This book is a contexture summary of some of the common issues that businesses face. The contents are prepared and presented from a personal perspective of what these common issues are, what works, and what you need to do to create and manage the right business for you and your team.

Enjoy the journey.

CHAPTER 1

Why and How We Learn

"You cannot teach a person anything;
You can only help him find it within himself."
Galileo Galilei

As individuals, we are constantly seeking to learn; to learn what we have to do to gain knowledge so that we can acquire new skills, improve ourselves and achieve more as we go through life.

This process is often described as the four stages of learning any new skill:

Stage 1

Unconscious Incompetence (UI)

Stage 2

Conscious Incompetence (CI)

Stage 3

Conscious Competence (CC)

Stage 4

Unconscious Competence (UC)

UI *Discovery*	*I don't know what I don't know*	☺
↓		
CI *Learnings*	*I know that I don't know*	☹
↓		
CC *Knowledge*	*I now know what I should know*	😐
↓		
UC *Skills*	*I know*	☺

From my coaching experience, the most important step is **Stage 1: Creating awareness from ignorance through self-discovery.** When a person is conscious of their ignorance, they are usually willing to learn, and quickly.

The process of coaching the skills they need is often a direct instruction of what they need to do: sharing the experience of what the outcomes are. When the skills and knowledge are acquired, a person moves quickly to practise the new skills for themselves, and to train others in the business.

In business, there are three distinct forms of learning: training, consulting and coaching.

Training involves the teaching of a specific skill set, whether technical skills or soft skills, to a person by instruction from a trainer, either internally or externally. All businesses need to train their employees in one form or another, at every stage as the business grows. When an issue is identified and the employees don't have the necessary skill set to resolve it, then they need to be trained. A trainer will deliver the training programme, teaching the employees the skill/s they need to learn. The training process is often delivered in an interactive workshop style, conducted in a classroom environment. The trainers teach. The employees learn.

Consulting is when an external party is invited to share their expertise on a specific matter. This might be to identify issues that are not working within a business and to provide the answers for the business to fix them. The normal process is for the consultant to carry out a fact-find and prepare a report with recommendations for the business to implement.

Consultancy is often used by corporate businesses, as it is perceived as the fastest and easiest way to solve problems by management. By appointing consultants, management delegate the responsibilities to an external source and, if the issues are not fixed, the consultants are to blame, not the business. My experience shows that many businesses find it difficult to implement the consultant's report, as they do not 'own' the report and so may not 'buy into' the recommendations. The outcome is that the report is shelved and left to gather dust over time, with little changes made. The expertise stays with the consultant and is not passed on to the business.

Coaching is a relatively new process which has been adopted by businesses over the past 30 years. Businesses are now more aware when they have an issue in their business, so they want to know what they need to do, themselves, to solve it. They often want external support to show them the process of how they can learn and what they need to do themselves. The coaching process is slower, as a coach will work with the business over a long period of time to identify the issues behind the problems. Many businesses consider coaching to be a 'softer' approach and, therefore, easier to adopt, as the self-learning is more applicable to themselves and the business. Many businesses need coaching, but not all businesses want to be coached.

This book is written from a coaching perspective to support individuals and businesses that want to learn. The outcomes of coaching are:

Business coaching transforms businesses.

Executive coaching transforms lives.

"The best business advice I ever received? Get a business coach."

Eric Schmidt, CEO Google

CHAPTER 2

The WHY Question

"People don't buy what you do, they buy why you do it."

Simon Sinek

The search for 'why' is a self-discovery journey for those who want to inspire themselves and others.

Simon Sinek said, "Great leaders have one thing in common. They start with the Why." Very few people in business can clearly articulate *why* they do what they do.

The question we need to ask ourselves is:

Why do I do what I do?

Why means "what is your purpose in business and in life?"

When asked what they do, most people can define the details of their job, their business, the challenges and the outcomes of their successes. However, when asked *why* they do what they do, most will pause and reflect on the meaning of the question, digging deeper into themselves and the real purpose of their business or their vision.

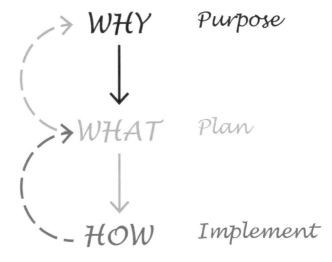

When a problem occurs in a business, the natural process is to identify what the issues are and prepare a plan for how to resolve them, often without knowing the source of the issues. However, by applying the Why question to the problem, we can go back to the source and identify the real problem that sits behind the issues. Many businesses understand what they do and how they do it, but only some understand *why* they do what they do.

Simon Sinek explains this clearly by comparing the success of two businesses, Dell and Apple. Dell's objective was to 'make and sell computers', i.e., *what* they do. Apple's objective was 'to solve problems through innovative design'. The outcome is that customers will only buy computers from Dell, while they will buy computers, music and telecommunication devices from Apple. Dell's sales of computers are driven by price, whereas Apple products are based on value – the Why question. Dell grew their business by making more computers, more powerful and cheaper. Apple grew their business by solving people's life problems through innovation.

The journey to discover the Why in any business often starts with the founder getting clear on the Why and the What. The journey is a self-discovery process in three parts:

My stories

The themes

Why statement

My Stories

Start with the founder's stories of their journey from childhood to now, including memorable experiences, and identify:

What are the stories that are special?

What are the experiences you loved?

What did you learn from these experiences?

How did these experiences affect you and who you have become?

Who makes a difference in your life?

The Themes

The next stage of this journey is to identify all the themes gathered from the stories. Themes are recurring ideas, words, phrases and feelings that emerge. Make a list of the themes you have identified.

Your list of themes may include:

To care

To create

To inspire

To motivate

Why Statement

From the themes listed, prepare some draft Why statements. These statements should be a sentence and consist of two parts: your **contribution** and the **impact**.

Refine the draft statements, allowing some time for reflection, before finalising your Why statements.

Some Why statements for a creative business could be:

To care about making the world better for people.

To care about making a positive difference to people's lives.

To care about wanting to make a difference.

CHAPTER 3

Staying in Context

Questions often asked:

What is context?

Why is it important in business?

What are the outcomes when a business understands context?

Understanding context is fundamental in business and yet, in my experience, this is often missed by business owners.

We spend most of our time managing the content of the business. Content is what happens inside a business, for example, attending to issues that require our immediate attention for the business to function and grow. Often, it is necessary to react to immediate issues, either externally from clients, or internally from employees.

When dealing with content, we can get lost in the detail of trying to solve issues in the 'how' space:

How do we solve this problem now?

How are we going to deal with this?

How do we do it now?

Sometimes, we ask ourselves the 'what' questions:

What do we need to do to solve the problem?

What do we need to do first?

What are the real issues?

Context puts us in a different headspace, helping us

understand *Why* we do what we do. In context, we respond to the problem differently, identifying the source issues by asking the Why questions:

Why do we need to do this?

Why is this necessary?

Why bother?

When operating in context, we get to the source of the issues faster and can respond more proactively.

The Context/Content model below illustrates the outcome:

Example – a fruit bowl. How do you select the right fruit to get the outcome you want?

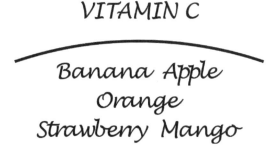

By setting the context for what we do in business, we

can achieve clarity and get to the source of issues faster, thus solving the problem sooner. Business owners who understand the context, and stay in context, will grow their business faster.

CHAPTER 4

The Business Cycle

Questions often asked:

What is a business cycle?

Why is it important to know about the business cycle?

Where is my business in the business cycle?

What is a business cycle?

Like the life cycle, the business cycle is a framework where business owners experience the journey of their business throughout its life. It is an emotional journey where the feelings are tracked from the beginning to the end.

Understanding these feelings will allow the owner to understand *why* they are feeling what they feel. It allows them to make decisions, plan ahead and expect the outcome they will achieve. Understanding others in the business and the effect they have is a vital part of managing a successful business.

Stages

The Stages framework, developed by Shirlaws (**www. shirlaws.com**), is one of many business-cycle models, but it is the only one that is based on the feelings of the owners/ employees at every stage of the journey.

The Stages framework is a diagram which illustrates the journey of the business through its life cycle. The framework is not time dependent. Different businesses will travel at different rates. Some may travel the whole life cycle in a few years, others may take decades.

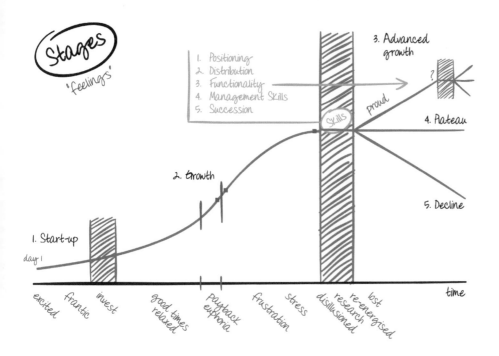

Businesses go through the following five stages in the business cycle:

1. Start-up
2. Growth
3. Advanced Growth

4. Plateau
5. Decline

1. Start-up

When a business is created, it is in the start-up stage. At the start of the business, the owner feels excited and creates a frantic energy as there is so much to do and not enough time to do everything. When the business acquires its first revenue, the feeling shifts to confidence – yes, the business works. The business then progresses to the '1st brick wall'. There is now a need to invest time and money to make the business operational, seek out business premises, recruit employees, etc.

2. Growth

With investment, the business progresses through the 1st brick wall stage onto the next stage of the cycle – growth. There are three phases of growth:

Good times – After the 1st brick wall, the frantic feeling has gone, the business grows and becomes consistently profitable. These successes create a 'good times' feeling, and the owner is more relaxed. The business will stay in the 'good times' phase and, with continued investment, will grow faster to the next stage.

Payback – A stage when the owner decides to reward themselves in recognition of all the hard work and time spent on getting the business to this stage successfully. Commercial paybacks, such as a salary increase and a new car, create a euphoric feeling of success.

2nd brick wall – The euphoria of payback in a business does not last, as the owners are often distracted from the business by its very success. This will result in the business not being managed efficiently by the owners, so frustration sets in. The owners feel stressed and the business enters the '2nd brick wall' phase. Employees can also feel tired, stressed and disillusioned. Sometimes, in this phase, the owners give up and sell, or exit from, the business. Years of hard work, growth and success are often thrown away when a business does not know how to get out of the 2nd brick wall phase.

3. Advanced Growth

When owners return to manage the business, they reinvest, restructure and re-energise it, shifting it out of the 2nd brick wall phase into 'advanced growth'. The five topics identified to shift the business into this stage are:

1. Positioning
2. Distribution
3. Functionality
4. Capability
5. Succession

Each of these topics is discussed later in the book. The feeling of the business in 'advanced growth' is one of pride; the owner is proud that the business has now shifted and is continuing to grow.

4. Plateau

When a business is not able to shift out of the 2nd brick wall stage, it will stagnate and eventually decline. The business owner feels lost and will seek to exit from the business.

5. Decline

Businesses in decline will eventually die or be purchased by others. Business owners feel worthless, as there is no value left in the business.

The next diagram is an example of a fact-find exercise, carried out to show that the professional business is in the 'growth' stage of the business cycle, but the directors are each at different stages, so their feelings are different from each other. This information enables the management team to make decisions with a clear understanding of each other.

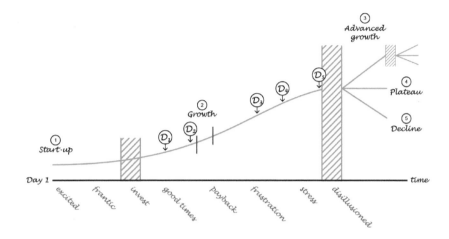

CHAPTER 5

The Business Model

Questions often asked:

What is a business model?

Why do I need to understand the model for my business?

Every business owner needs to understand the concept of a business model and how it can be applied to their business. The business model is a framework applicable to all businesses. By adopting the framework, different businesses will develop their own model that best suits them, in order to grow.

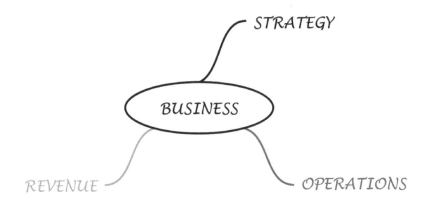

A business model is a simple diagram explaining what a business needs to do for the employees to operate with a clear understanding of what they do and where the business is going. The basic model consists of three parts linked together: Strategy, Revenue and Operations.

Every business needs Revenue and Operations.

Over time, if the Revenue is greater than the Operations, the business is in profit. A profitable business is the first stage of a successful business. As long as the business remains profitable, it can and will grow. If the Operations cost is greater than the Revenue, the business is making a loss and will not survive. I describe this as a Blue Red business model.

Revenue

This is the most important function when starting a business. Its objective is to create income. The contents of some revenue functions are products, positioning, sales and referrals.

Operations

This is the functional part of the business that allows it to create revenue. The contents of an operational function are staff, premises, IT, infrastructure, finance and management.

When a business has established its Revenue and Operations, it will seek to look into the future in order to create a legacy, long after the owners have departed.

Strategy

Smart businesses focus on growing the business and creating a long-term legacy. The contents of some strategic functions are vision, succession and valuation.

Culture

Culture is the glue that binds the whole business together. Every business has a culture, whether it is stated or not. The culture is the business. It is what the business is and what it represents. Many successful businesses define their culture explicitly and are proud of their values, for example, **www.zappos.com/about/**

A business with a clearly defined model that operates within the framework is a functional business, which is *right* for the business. The right business creates great outcomes for the owners and employees – they are happy, enjoy working in the business and will contribute to growing the business more than expected.

An example of a detailed business model, developed by a professional business, is shown opposite:

	STRATEGY	REVENUE	OPERATIONS	CULTURE
CONTEXT	Vision	Energy	Responsibilities	Alignment
CONTENT	Growth Strategy Succession plan	Core products Market positioning Sales/referrer	Structure Capacity Right people	Core values Behaviours Activities
OUTCOME	Work-life balance High valuation	Clients buy Value products High client retention	Efficient Communicative Right profit	Love business Happy staff Loyal clients

CHAPTER 6

Creating Revenue

"Revenue is Vanity; Profit is Sanity; Cash is Reality."

Unknown

Questions often asked:

What is the right revenue for my business?

Why is it important to generate the right type of revenue, not any revenue?

What does the right revenue look like in my business?

Revenue is generated in a business when a client pays a sum of money for the delivery of a product. The fundamental principle of any business is to generate revenue. Without revenue, most businesses will not survive. When you start a business, the first thing you need to do is get a client, sell your product, deliver your product, receive payment and make a profit. Repeat this process and you will continue to grow your business.

There are four main components of the revenue model:

Product

The product is the foundation of the business. It is what the business sells, and the clients buy. Every business starts with a product to sell to the market. The business will grow as you sell more of the same product to more clients. As the business continues to grow, different products are created. These may be extensions of existing products or new products.

Positioning

The positioning of a product is defined by the cost and services provided by the business, in comparison to other similar products in the marketplace. Many businesses will position their product to create a uniqueness, which stands out from its competitors, and will thus create more sales. A product with a clearly defined position in the marketplace will grow fast.

Sales

A sale occurs when a business brings a product to the marketplace. All businesses need to sell their products, either directly to prospects and clients, or through distributions and referrers. A physical product sale to a customer is based on the costs and/or value. A service sale to clients is based on the relationships created between the business and its clients.

Referrers

A referral is when a client comes to you to buy your product. The referrer process is more relevant to service businesses where the product has been recommended by one client to another business or person, resulting in a sale. A business with a defined referral process grows faster because the clients come to you.

We will review, in detail, how each of these components is related and what a business needs to understand in order to grow.

A contexture summary of the revenue framework is shown below:

	PRODUCT	POSITIONING	SALES	REFERRERS
CONTEXT	Foundation	Focus	Create relationship	Manage relationship
CONTENT	The physical product or a service your business sells	Where the product is in the marketplace	What the business needs to do to sell the products	What the business needs to do to attract clients to buy your product
OUTCOME	Cost vs value	Differential from the crowd	More revenue	Fast growth

Right Revenue

The right revenue created for the business has three components:

Right	=	Right	+	Right	+	Right
Revenue		Products		Clients		Cost

The **right products** are the core products that the business produces, which the market needs and/or wants.

The **right clients** are the clients who want to buy the product, for the right price, at the right time.

The **right cost** is what the clients pay to receive the benefits of the products.

Positioning

Every business has a position in the marketplace. Positioning is what makes the business stand out from its competitors, often based on the product it sells. Clients may view all businesses and products to be similar, until a business defines its position. When a business grows, it often needs to reposition where it wants to be.

The outcomes of a business with a clearly defined position are:

Attracting the right clients to buy the products.

Recognition as the expert in the marketplace.

Products that are based on value not cost.

To create the right position for your business, ask yourself:

What makes your product different from your competitors?

How are you perceived in the marketplace?

What position do you need to change to, to create growth?

Positioning Strategy

There are three scenarios for any business:

If your business does not have a position in the marketplace, you need to **create** a position.

If you are not clear on your position in the marketplace, you need to **build** a position.

If your business is growing and changing its products, you need to **reposition** your business in the marketplace.

Positioning Your Business

A business needs to be clear of its positioning relating to its product, service and price. For example:

Product - Is the quality of your product better, the

same as or worse than your competitors?

Service - Is the service you provide average, better or worse compared to others?

Price – Is your product perceived as expensive, of average price or cheap?

Note: No business can deliver a product that is great, of excellent service and cheap.

Position Matrix

There are 16 boxes to define where your business position is in the marketplace:

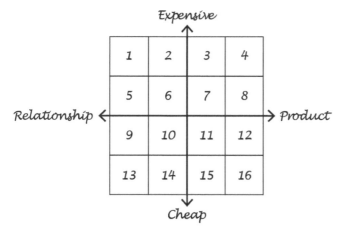

What are the criteria for defining your products?

Are you selling your products based on quality?

Are you selling your products based on the service you provide?

Are your products perceived as expensive or cheap?

By positioning your business in one of the 16 boxes, you will define:

Where your business is in the marketplace.

Where your clients and competitors are.

Complete this exercise with your top clients, suppliers and competitors; it will give you a clear picture of where your business is.

If your business is in a box where there are few competitors, then you are in command of the marketplace.

If your business is in a box with many of its competitors, then the market is crowded and you may wish to move to another position.

If your clients and suppliers are in the same box or near you, then they are aligned with your business and you will continue to grow your business with these clients and suppliers.

If your clients are not in the same box or near you, then your businesses are not aligned and you will not continue to sell to these businesses for long.

If your business has defined its vision to grow, you may wish to review where you want to be and reposition your business accordingly.

The example below of a professional business position in the marketplace shows they are in Box 6. They have the opportunity to grow their business to the adjoining positions with their products:

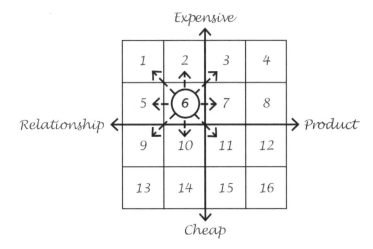

Products

All businesses need products to sell to their clients. A product can be either a physical piece of equipment, for example, a computer, or a service, such as legal advice.

A product-based business is focused on product research and development to produce a unique product for the market.

A service-based business is focused on developing a strong relationship with their clients to create loyalty.

Core Products

Core products are the main products in a business that generate its major revenue. An established business will have a range of core products. Service businesses will focus on a range of four to seven core products. Where a business has less than four core products, it is at a higher risk if one product does not generate the revenue as forecasted. A business with more than seven core products will have difficulty positioning itself in the marketplace. It will be perceived as a 'jack of all trades and master of none'. Businesses that have many core products often separate these products into separate businesses but remain part of the group of businesses. This allows each business to focus on their core products and to grow.

Most start-up businesses begin by selling one product to the market. The pace of growth of the business will depend on how fast the product is sold to clients. The strategy for increasing a product sale is to identify similar prospects who want to buy.

As the client base is established, the next stage is to sell more to the same clients. As the business grows, the sales strategy is to identify bigger clients or prospects who want to buy more of the same product, and more often. From the success of the sales, you can then ask the clients for referrals to others who will benefit from buying your products. A strong referrer will create a hot sale and will grow your business.

PRODUCT	TOP CLIENTS	TOP PROSPECTS	TOP REFERRERS
Core Product 1	Client 1	Prospect 1 Prospect 2 Prospect 3	Referrer 1 Referrer 2 Referrer 3
	Client 2	Prospect 4 Prospect 5 Prospect 6	Referrer 4 Referrer 5 Referrer 6
	Client 3	Prospect 7 Prospect 8 Prospect 9	Referrer 7 Referrer 8 Referrer 9

The process of identifying top clients who will refer prospects will create business growth. In summary:

Top clients normally generate 80% of revenue.

Top prospects referred by clients create a hot sale.

Top referrers are clients who are happy with the product and keen to tell others about its benefits.

Product Extensions

Many businesses will have the opportunity to review their core products and identify which core products (P1, P2 and P3) should be extended (PE1, PE2, PE3...PE9) as part of its offering:

$$P1 \longrightarrow PE1 \qquad P2 \longrightarrow PE4 \qquad P3 \longrightarrow PE7$$
$$\longrightarrow PE2 \qquad \longrightarrow PE5 \qquad \longrightarrow PE8$$
$$\longrightarrow PE3 \qquad \longrightarrow PE6 \qquad \longrightarrow PE9$$

An example of a business selling home furniture might extend its product range to sell office furniture, garden furniture and/or hotel furniture, etc.

Creating product extensions is a natural, fast way for a business to grow.

It will enable the business to sell more products to clients and prospects.

Having product extensions is an easy, low-cost route to create a range of products for different clients in different markets.

Using the referral process will expand sales calls to different prospects, for example:

> Client refers to similar types of prospects. Prospects buy P1, P2 and P3.

> Client refers to different types of prospects. Prospects buy P1, P2, P3, PE1, PE2 and PE3.

New Products

Many businesses grow by creating new products in addition to their core products. These might be products that are not yet available in the business, but which have been identified as what the market needs, for example:

House Builder: Core Product – Housing Construction

New Product 1 – Housing development

New Product 2 – Housing finance

When a business grows beyond a manageable size, it will need to restructure into different groups of businesses, with different new products, for example:

Existing Construction Company:

Group 1 – Commercial construction

Group 2 – Residential construction

Group 3 – Infrastructure construction

Each group will have its own core products, product extensions and new products under a holding group. See the example below of a construction business:

BUSINESS HOLDING GROUP			
Market Sector	Commercial	Residential	Infrastructure
Core Product (CP)	Office construction	Housing construction	Road construction
Product Extensions (PE)	Hotel construction Hospital construction	Nursing home construction Student accommodation	Motorway construction
New Products (NP)	Office development Commercial loans	Housing development Housing mortgages	Airport construction Infrastructure construction

Understanding Revenue: Clients, Prospects and Referrers

Revenue is the outcome of a business that sells its product/services to:

Clients – who buy and pay.

Prospects – who you want to be your client.

Referrers – who can introduce you to prospects.

The revenue framework below explains the context, content, process, outcome and pace of creating revenue:

REVENUE FRAMEWORK			
	Clients	**Prospects**	**Referrers**
Context	Loyalty	Create Relationships	Manage Relationships
Content	Standard and Extra	6 Step Sales Call Process	6 Step Referrers Call Process
Process	Client Loyalty Programme	4 Touch Sales Strategy	4 Touch Referrer Strategy
Outcome	Revenue	Clients	Clients/Prospects
Pace	Fast	Medium	Slow

Clients

Clients are the most important revenue generator for any business, as they have already bought and paid for the product/services. The clients have knowledge of the product, the price they paid and the value they received.

To create more revenue faster, a business needs to sell more of the same products to their clients and introduce other product extensions and new products. In many businesses, the 80/20 rule applies – 80% of the revenue is generated from 20% of the clients. If you focus on the top 20% of your client base and prepare a loyalty programme to provide extra services specifically for them, you will then have created a loyal client base in which your business will grow as their business grows.

To create a loyalty programme for your business, you need to:

1. Identify the top 20% of your client base, based on revenue.
2. Identify the core products they buy and other product sales.
3. Understand their culture and the values that you both share.
4. Prepare a 12-month loyalty programme with activities to manage client loyalty.
5. Implement the loyalty programme.

Prospects

Prospects are potential clients who want to buy your product because they need it for their own business. If you are selling your product to a prospect, you need to be clear that the product is what the prospect wants. Prior to selling, you need to create a relationship with your prospects.

The traditional sales process consists of three stages:

1. Meet and talk to 10 prospects.
2. Arrange at least three appointments for a sales call.
3. Convert at least one prospect to a client.

Sales Calls

Professional sales calls are defined with a process to create a higher sales conversion. The Six Step sales call process, illustrated by Shirlaws, is shown as an example below:

Step 1	Agenda: Set a specific agenda for the sales call.
Step 2	Position: Clarify the position of the prospect. Check if the prospect has been referred and if this is a pre-sold meeting.
Step 3	Fact-find/feel-find: Conduct a fact-find about their business. Conduct a feel-find by asking questions to ascertain the feelings in the business. Pause.
Step 4	Presentation: Present the product visually to create a need.
Step 5	Summary: Prospects normally ask three questions: How does it work? What will it cost? When can I buy?
Step 6	Open: Agree what's next for the prospect and you.

Sales Strategy

A sales strategy is a plan which identifies all the prospects, with a programme to keep in touch (four touches) over a period of time. The plan allows you to record and plan whom you need to meet again and when.

The outcome for each touch could be:

> A successful sale and the prospect becomes a client.
>
> Arrange another date for a second sales call.
>
> Remove the prospect from the plan, as your values do not match.

Solution Sales

Smart businesses do not just sell their products but identify products specifically to sell to their clients to suit their needs. This is defined as a 'solution sale'. A solution sale is often identified in the fact-find stage of the sales call. A solution sale is not upselling.

For example:

> The client wants to buy a TV (Product sell).
>
> The client is sold additional products to complement the TV (Upsell).
>
> The client does not know they want a TV (Solution sell).

The Six Step process for a solution sales call is different from a sales call. The first stage in a solution sale is to carry out a detailed fact-find process and identify what the prospect's source issues are in their business.

Questions asked of the client are often related to the Why: *Why do you want to…?*

Listening carefully to the client will allow you to identify the real issues in their business and then propose a solution. By identifying the source issues, you have identified the true need of the client and, therefore, you can sell the right product for the client's need.

Referrals

The purpose of referrals is to source prospects and clients that the business doesn't know. If a business wants to grow, referrals are the key to continuous growth.

Referrals are about creating relationships with clients and third parties, and managing these relationships well. The benefits of a strong business relationship are that the referrers will:

Increase their own revenue with repeat business.

Improve loyalty between both parties.

Gain knowledge in the industry and marketplace.

Referrals are also about understanding fear. Many businesses are fearful about referring their clients to another business due to a lack of trust, control, quality, integrity and time. If you can manage these and emphasise the benefits instead, your clients will refer your business to others. A strong referrer creates a pre-sold sales call, where the prospect wants to buy.

The Referral Process

The referral process consists of four stages:

Stage 1 – Phone call or email to arrange a meeting.

Stage 2 – Meet to assess shared values.

> If there are shared values, proceed to the next stage.

> If there are no shared values, end the relationship.

Stage 3 – Carry out a fact-find and discuss fears and benefits.

Stage 4 – Implement and start referring.

Referral calls are similar to sales calls, as the desired outcome is to win a new client. When you have created and managed strong relationships with your clients, you will receive a continuous stream of new prospects and referrers, and your business will continue to grow.

CHAPTER 7

A Functional Business

"A team is not a group of people who work together.

A team is a group of people who trust each other."

Simon Sinek

Questions often asked:

What is a functional business?

How do I create and manage a functional business?

Why is effective communication essential in a functional business?

A functional business is like a car that is well-designed, runs smoothly, is maintained regularly and is fun to drive.

Functionality is about the operations in a business – how it works in day-to-day operation, who does what, who reports to whom, and how you communicate effectively with each other within the business.

What do you need to create a functional business?

A functional business consists of three complementary components:

Functional = Right	+	Right	+	Right
Business		Capacity	Capabilities	Structure

The **right capacity** is the right number of employees, providing maximum efficiency with minimum effort.

The **right capabilities** in a business are the right people, with the right skills required for the business to function and grow.

The **right structure** is the relationship between everyone in the business to facilitate the right responsibilities, reporting and communication with each other.

The model for creating a business structure consists of two parts:

Shareholders

Employees (including management)

Shareholders

Shareholders are the owners of the business. In a start-up or small business, the owners often work in the business and sometimes own 100% of it. In medium and large businesses, some shareholders are investors and they do not work in the business.

Corporate businesses have a board of shareholders whose objective is to maximise the Return on Investment (ROI) and their main responsibility is to appoint the right CEO or MD. A profitable, successful business will pay the shareholders' annual dividends. Dividend payment is related to profitability.

Management

The management of a small business is often the owner, self-appointed as the CEO or MD. In an SME, there will be a board of directors, each with a specific responsibility in the management of the business.

The objective of the board of directors is to create a vision for the business to grow and increase profitability. The role of the CEO or MD is to provide the right leadership to energise the board, create a strong culture and increase the ROI for shareholders.

Directors are remunerated with a salary based on their roles and responsibility, plus a bonus based on their individual and business performances.

Leadership and the roles and responsibilities of a leader

A leader's roles and responsibilities include:

Creating a clear vision for the business to grow.

Recruiting the right people with the right capabilities and empowering them to grow the business.

Creating a strong culture in which everyone shares the values.

Operations

Operations in a business consist of a wide range of day-to-day activities, including staff recruitment and retention, premises, infrastructure, administration, finance, etc.

The top three components that create a right business are:

Right	=	Right	+	Right	+	Right
Business		People		Finance		Structure

The expected outcomes of a right business are:

The right people, happy doing the right job.

Improved job satisfaction by empowering employees, with clear areas of self-responsibilities.

Predictable forecast of resource allocation in the business.

Right People

"Surround yourself with the right people."
Tony Hsieh, entrepreneur and ex-CEO of Zappos

Questions often asked:

What is my real job in the business?

What do I do and what should I do?

Who does what?

The Three Areas of Business

A functional business consists of three components:

Strategy – Vision, Succession, Valuation

Revenue – Product, Positioning, Sales, Referrals

Operations – Staff Resources, Premises, Finance, Management

Roles and Responsibilities (RR)

Individual RR:

> Prepare a document for each individual employee, stating what their role is and what they are responsible for in the business.

Group RR:

> Create a summary of each group's RR – e.g. Management Board, Revenue Team, Operations Team.

Outcome:

> Clarity of individuals' and groups' RR will ensure there are no gaps. This will also allow forward planning and advance allocation of different functions.

Below is an example of an MD's RR from a professional business:

ROLE	RESPONSIBILITIES
STRATEGY	
Capacity planning & management	Manage strategy for growth Prepare succession strategy
Referral	Manage referral system
Client management	Manage new/existing clients
Positioning	Review opportunities with existing clients
New products	Research opportunities and market trends
REVENUE	
Operations management	Manage business revenue and spend Review team/project profitability
Sales	Create new opportunities & increase profile Co-ordinate submissions and pitches Strategically identify attendance at events
Marketing	Review the application of intelligence and research Coordinate specific areas of research
Initialise projects	Brief key staff and set expectations
Project delivery	Review and sign off design Publish design review protocol
Client services	Post completion feedback & referrals
OPERATIONS	
Administration	Capacity plan implementation
Secretarial	Responsible for all admin staff
Accounting & finance	Review budgets and approve expenditure and funding Manage accounts, forecast, fees, and debtors/creditors. Manage fee and resource allocation Liaise with company accountant and sign off accounts
Premises	Leases and rental agreements

Human resources	Review and update Roles and Responsibilities of staff Senior staff recruitment Performance review and remuneration Responsible for staff disciplinary procedures and redundancy
Legal	Liaise with advisors on business issues
Compliance	Ensure accounts published
CULTURE	
Activities	Cultural alignment across whole business

Red Blue **Black (RBB)** %

When analysing the % of resources spent in each area of the business – Strategy (black), Revenue (blue) and Operations (red) – the management team will know what each individual and group are doing and how this will impact the performance, efficiency and profitability of the business.

Individual RBB%:

> Record actual % of each employee's time spent in each area of activity. Assess and change these % allocations as required.

Group RBB%:

> Summary of the % of the total group's time spent in each area of activity in the whole business.

Outcome:

> Clarity of the actual % time spent by each employee and group.

> Understanding the efficiency and profitability of the business.

> Opportunity to change and improve.

STAFF TIME ALLOCATION	STRATEGY	REVENUE	OPERATIONS
Staff 1 Staff 2 Staff 3			
Total			
Average %			

Finance

There are two parts to understanding business finance: Profit and Loss (P&L) and Cash Flow Forecast.

Profit and Loss (P&L)

This is an actual record of the past 12 months of revenue, employee costs, overheads, profits and cash position of the business.

The context of preparing a P&L statement is for the business to know and understand its performance, to learn what works and what could be done differently.

Cash Flow Forecast

This is the predicted forecast of the next 12 months of revenue, employee costs, overheads, profits and cash position of the business, based on recurring expenses and transactions.

The context of a Cash Flow Forecast is to allow the business to predict and understand where the business will be in the next 12 months and to take appropriate action.

Organisational Structure

Questions often asked:

> What is an organisational structure?
>
> Why does my business need a structure?
>
> What is the right structure for my business?

An organisational structure shows how people and activities are organised to achieve the business's goals. These activities are included in the individual RR. The objective is to allow quick decision-making and to facilitate direct communication between the employees.

The organisational structure of your business reflects how you work and communicate with each other. Most businesses start without a structure and continue to grow until the employees find it difficult to communicate effectively. Maybe they are not sure whom they should report to or whom they should ask about an issue.

There are two fundamental types of organisational structure: informal and formal.

An **informal** structure has no written document that defines the rules, regulations and communication line. Employees rely on relationships forged with each other and depend on cooperation from those who work best with them. This structure is highly adaptable and can work well for up to 12 people in a business. After that, it becomes difficult to increase the number of employees until a formal structure is in place.

A **formal** structure is a written or published diagram, explaining how things work within the business. It is often illustrated to show direct lines of responsibility and communication between management and staff, thus preventing any misunderstanding. This establishes a method of decision-making and a process for implementation. Many traditional and corporate businesses show a hierarchical pyramid. Other businesses are now exploring different structures. The three most common types of formal structure are Flat, Pyramid and Collaborative.

From my coaching experience, small businesses that grow into larger businesses develop a structure that works for them, often through a process of discussion and contribution from all employees.

CHAPTER 8

Vision: The Purpose in Business

"The future depends on what you do today."
Mahatma Gandhi

Questions often asked:

What is vision and what does it mean in business?

Why do businesses need a vision?

How do I create a vision in my business?

Vision in business stimulates growth through emotional engagement by staff. Often, visions in businesses are just goal statements, with a long-term dateline that lacks motivation.

Vision is part of Strategy in the business model. Smart businesses use vision to create a strong desire among their employees to be part of a successful, growing business, which achieves an outcome beyond their expectations, making them proud of their contribution towards it.

A clear vision provides clarity and is about the feelings in the business that motivate employees to feel good today and even better in the future. Clients buy from businesses that have a clear vision of why they do what they do.

There are two components, as illustrated in the vision model opposite:

Core Purpose – defines the commercial aspiration of the business, which creates an impact and contribution to the world.

Core Values – defines the culture of the business relating to the employees, which states who we are, what we stand for and why we are here.

The process of finding the core purpose and core values of a business is often carried out by a third-party facilitator, starting with the founder, then the senior management team and the whole business.

Core Purpose

The core purpose of a business is the fundamental reason for being in the business. It is often defined as the intent of the founder or founders who lead the business.

A business's core purpose is a statement that describes the founder's aspiration and motivates the employees, which in turn creates an impact on the world. It captures the soul of the business. The core purpose is like a guiding star, forever pursued, inspiring and living. It does not change but inspires change. The outcome for a business is constant progress and change, living its purpose to the full.

The process for creating a business's core purpose needs to be facilitated by a third party or coach who is not in the business and has no attachment to the management and staff. The process can be carried out with the founder and/or the senior management team. Depending on the size and type of business, the process is carried out in three stages, as explained in *Find Your Why* by Simon Sinek:

Share the experiences:

Review and recapture stories of the founder's personal and business life, of what they did, what has been memorable and what creates an impact in their life.

Identify the themes:

Capture the core facts of the stories, the feelings/emotions and the impact this has had on the founder's life.

Define the Why:

Identify the overarching themes and prepare a draft statement beginning with: *To…(contribute)…, so that…(impact)…*

Implementing the Core Purpose

On the completion of the Why statement, the next stage is to incorporate this into the whole business with full buy-in from the employees and to start the implementation.

How is this carried out?

Share the experiences, themes and the Why statement with all employees.

Prepare a list of actions for all employees to understand and fully buy in, be responsible and live the Why.

Core Values

The core values of a business are the values that are important to the employees in the business, which are exhibited in their behaviours. The process to define the core values in a business is described in Chapter 9: Culture, What Culture?

Vision Picture

"Live your vision now."

Darren Shirlaw

Questions often asked:

> What is a vision picture?
>
> What does it mean and what does it look like in business?
>
> Why do businesses need a vision picture?

A vision picture is a business strategy that visually illustrates the journey of where the business is going from now to a date in the future. Unlike most business strategies, a vision picture is a living and feeling strategy where all employees can connect and relate to where the business is now and its future journey.

When does a business need a vision picture?

This depends on where the business is in the business cycle. A start-up business will focus on creating revenue and growing the team. A business only needs to create a vision picture when it is in the growth stage, when the owners pause to reflect and ask, 'What is the purpose of the business?', 'Why are we doing what we are doing?' and, 'Where are we going?'

What does a vision picture look like?

A vision picture is a simple diagram showing where the business is now and where it wants to be in the future.

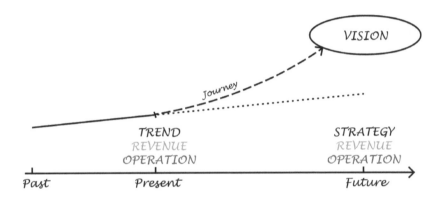

The period from now until a date in the future will depend on the number of founders/owners, their ages and when they wish to exit from the business. This period is usually between 5 to 10 years. For many businesses, a period of less than 5 years may be difficult to achieve exponential growth. A future date of over 10 years will not be attractive to most owners, as it feels too distant to relate to.

How do you create a vision picture?

A vision picture has two main parts:

> The trend – A record of the business over the past years.

> The strategy – What the business wants to achieve from now, over a certain period.

Trend

The trend of a business is the data collected over a period of time on revenue generated, staff and overhead costs, and profits.

Revenue trend:

Turnover: £, %, and % increase

Products: number of core products

Clients: number of key clients, revenue generated per client

Sales: number of sales calls, conversion ratio

Referrals: number of referrals, sales conversion ratio

Operations trend:

Staff: number of staff, % increase pa

Staff costs: total costs pa % of turnover

Overhead costs: total costs pa, % of turnover

Profit: profit pa % of turnover, % increase/decrease

Trend and Strategy

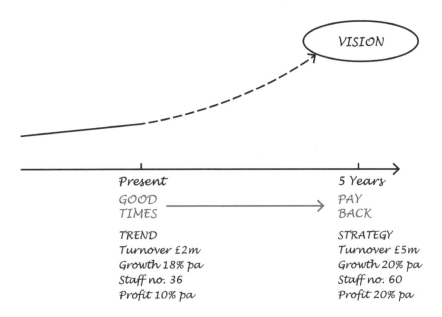

The above illustration is of a business trend and strategy over a period of five years, with the following trends:

Revenue trend:

Turnover increased by 18% pa i.e. doubled over five years

Number of core clients doubled every five years

Number of core products doubled every five years

Operations trend:

Number of staff doubled every five years

Staff costs doubled every five years

Overhead costs are 25% of annual turnover

Profit is 10% of turnover

The trend shows that this is a successful, profitable and growing business in 'good times'.

Present

Prior to preparing the business strategy, it is essential to identify the contexture information on the following:

Turnover per annum

Revenue generated from each core product

Revenue generated from each key client, on each core product

Number of staff

Total staff cost, % of turnover

Total overhead costs, % of turnover

Future

The proposal for the strategy of the business will be defined by the management team, based on their feelings about what they want to achieve and where they want to be after a certain period of time. This is often guided by the % growth of the business, based on the trend. Three options for discussion are:

Normal growth – based on the trend growth rate pa

Medium growth – 1½ to 2 times above the trend pa

Fast growth – 3+ times above the trend pa

On the selection of an option, the business can prepare a forecast on the strategy with contexture data of the size of the business, what it looks like and how it feels to be in the business.

CHAPTER 9

Culture, What Culture?

"Where there is love, there is life."

Mahatma Gandhi

Questions often asked:

What is culture?

Why is culture important in business?

How do I create the right culture in my business?

What is culture?

Culture is often defined by the way the business does its business. Clients observe the services they receive through the employees' behaviours in delivering the products. Culture often manifests through employees' behaviours, both inside and outside the business.

All businesses have a culture, whether stated or not. A business creates the culture by defining its core values based on what is important to them, what behaviours they want for their staff and what activities reflect their values.

Why is culture important in business?

A business that defines its culture creates a strong functional business where everyone works together towards the vision. The outcome is a happy, loyal team, where everyone is energised and takes full responsibility for what they do, individually and together.

A strong culture will create a successful, profitable and happy business. Staff love working in the business. Clients love buying from the business. An example of a successful business that has a strong culture is Zappos.

How do I create the right culture in my business?

Culture often starts with the owners and is defined by their personal values and behaviours through their activities. As a business grows, it may change the culture through a process of sharing, discussing and defining what is important to the founders, management and the people who work there, both individually and as a group.

There are three stages to creating a business culture.

Stage 1 – Identify Core Values

The first stage is to define its core values, which are important to the employees in the business:

What inspires the employees to work in the business?

What is important to the owners?

What makes a good work environment?

The process of defining a business's core values is to engage all the employees to participate in a workshop where they can contribute to the exercise. Start by identifying personal values that are important to each individual. Gather all the individual values, and then explore and identify the values that are common to all.

Through this process of sharing, discussing and debating what values are important and why, the group will identify a set of values, between three and six, which are familiar to everyone. These are the business's core values.

Stage 2 – Define Behaviours and Monitor

For each core value, every employee will define their personal behaviours that reflect the value. From these behaviours, the group will share, discuss and agree on a list of behaviours that are acceptable in their business.

This list of behaviours is then published for all employees to monitor themselves, and each other, over a set period of time. If the behaviours come naturally to everyone, it confirms that the values are the right core values for the business. If the majority of employees find it difficult to behave as stated, then the value in question may not be relevant to the business and should be discarded. Managing and monitoring self-behaviour over a period of time is a test for the individual to reflect whether they are aligned with others and whether they fit into the business or not.

An outcome of this exercise can often lead to some employees leaving the business, as they realise that they do not fit into the culture of the business and will feel uncomfortable if they continue to work there.

Stage 3 – Create Activities

For each core value, the group will prepare a list of activities that reflect what they do together in the business, regularly. These activities, business and social, strengthen the business culture and confirm its core values.

An example of the culture, core values, behaviours and activities developed by a design business is illustrated on the next page:

CORE VALUES	BEHAVIOURS	PRESENT ACTIVITIES	PROPOSED ACTIVITIES
RESPECT	We are trustworthy. We are honest. We are committed.	We respect each other and work as a team. We meet each week to discuss our work. We make the most of individual skills.	We will prepare a staff handbook. We will respond to all queries within 4 hours. We will provide new staff with an induction programme.
BALANCE	We enjoy a flexible work-life balance. We value our relationships. We have fun.	We work ½ day on Fridays. We spend time with each other outside the business. We engage in social activities together.	We will organise regular social events with partners. We will organise social outings once a month. We will share our workload.
CREATIVITY	We love to design. We are creative. We enjoy problem-solving.	We review our design regularly. We discuss and review all projects. We organise visits to events in the creative sphere.	We will share design ideas with everyone. We will hold project reviews monthly. We will update our Pinterest page regularly.

My experience of three professional businesses that have developed, built and implemented the right culture for their businesses are:

Threesixty Architecture – **www.360architecture.com**

LBA – **www.studiolba.co.uk**

LMA – **www.l-m-a.co.uk**

CHAPTER 10

Living in the New Paradigm

"People don't care how much you know until they know how much you care."

Theodore Roosevelt

Questions often asked:

Who are you?

What is the new paradigm?

How do I live in the new paradigm?

Who are You?

This is certainly not a question many of us ask ourselves or even understand why we need to ask. Yet it is a very personal, important question that all of us should ask ourselves at some point in our life and in business.

From my coaching experience, this topic surfaces in an executive coaching session when a client's business is facing a major issue which will change the client's life.

By asking this question, the process will take the client to a personal space of reflection and review, helping them to understand the true source issues in their life that are affecting their business. Often, it is difficult, sometimes impossible, to support a client until this question is answered.

Be True to Yourself

In business, as in life, we are constantly preoccupied with doing more and doing better so we feel 'good enough'. This is driven by the false belief that who we are is not good enough. We hope that by doing enough, doing more, doing better, one day we will feel good enough, we will feel valued, recognised, loved, and we will be OK.

An understanding of the paradigm we live in will support us: who we are, where we are and where we want to be.

The Paradigm

We live in a world of two paradigms: the Old and the New, as presented by Rosslyn Tasker of Inugo Coaching.

When we live in the Old paradigm, we live in a Fear space feeling:

> I am not good enough.
>
> I am not valuable.
>
> I am not loveable.

When we live in the New paradigm, we live in a Love space feeling:

> I am well, loveable and valuable.

I manage my own energy.

I create the whole of my own reality.

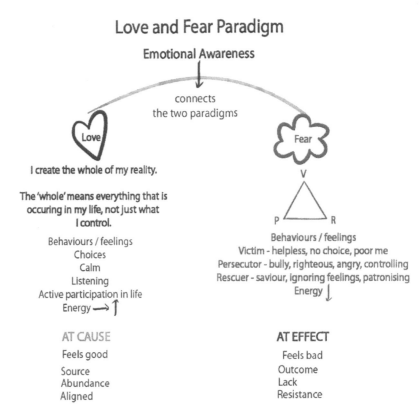

Love and Fear Paradigm

Emotional Awareness

connects
the two paradigms

Love

Fear

I create the whole of my reality.

The 'whole' means everything that is
occuring in my life, not just what
I control.

Behaviours / feelings
Choices
Calm
Listening
Active participation in life
Energy ⟶ ↑

P   R

Behaviours / feelings
Victim - helpless, no choice, poor me
Persecutor - bully, righteous, angry, controlling
Rescuer - saviour, ignoring feelings, patronising
Energy ↓

AT CAUSE

Feels good

Source
Abundance
Aligned

AT EFFECT

Feels bad

Outcome
Lack
Resistance

A paradigm is the basic way of perceiving, thinking, valuing and doing associated with
a particular vision of reality.

Open Up

The Open Up process is a coaching process to support a person in understanding and shifting from the Old paradigm to the New paradigm. This is carried out in three stages:

Stage 1 – Love myself now.

Stage 2 – Tell the whole truth now.

Stage 3 – Be self-responsible now.

The outcome: **I create the whole of my own reality.**

Stage 1: Love Myself Now

When we live in the Old paradigm, we live in the Fear space, either as a victim, persecutor or rescuer. In the New paradigm, we live in the Love space, loving, sharing and caring for ourselves and others.

The process of shifting from the Old to the New paradigm can be carried out in three parts:

Part 1: Acknowledge all self-feelings in the Old paradigm as a victim, persecutor or rescuer. List all fear behaviours such as:

I blame...

I destroy...

I worry...

Part 2: Discover self-feelings in the New paradigm in the loving, caring and sharing space. List all love behaviours such as:

I understand...

I trust...

I inspire...

Part 3: Monitor self-feelings and behaviours regularly. When one feels and behaves in the fear space, look up the list of the opposite feeling and change one's self-behaviour accordingly, such as:

I blame ⟶ *I understand*

This responsive action will shift us from the Old to the New paradigm instantly. By practising this process and shifting self-behaviour regularly, you will unconsciously:

Love myself now

Stage 2: Tell the Whole Truth Now

When we tell our truth, we often do not tell the whole truth. Only you know when you are telling the truth in part or full. Telling the whole truth is an understanding of yourself without fear or judgement and an acknowledgement of yourself living in the New paradigm.

When you know you are telling the truth, but not the whole truth, you need to reflect and respond to yourself to tell the whole truth. The process of telling the whole truth to yourself requires regular practice, monitoring and self-correction. When this is recognised and corrected in the moment, the feeling of fear disappears, and love comes to you.

By practising this iterative process regularly, you will feel the love of yourself and be living in the New paradigm. There is no ego attached and there is no mask to hide behind.

Stage 3: Be Self-Responsible

By telling the whole truth to yourself, you will take responsibility and choose who you are, what you want to be and how you want to live your life.

Decisions made by you will create the outcome:

I create the whole of my own reality

CHAPTER 11

Communication

"People will forget what you said, people will forget what you did,

but people will never forget how you made them feel."

Maya Angelou

Questions often asked:

> What is good communication?
>
> Why is good communication important in business?
>
> How do I improve communication in business?

Communication is fundamental for all of us, both in business and in our personal lives. The bigger the business, the bigger the challenge for effective communication. We are not often aware when our message has been heard, understood or misinterpreted. Many of us may not have a clear understanding of our own communication style, or that of others.

How We Communicate

Communication can be explained by this simple diagram between the sender and the receiver:

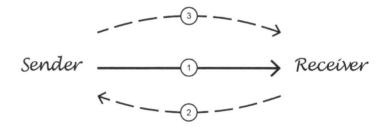

In my experience, half the messages we send are not clearly understood or received. This can be rectified by the following process:

1. After the message is sent, the sender asks the receiver to confirm the message.

2. The receiver confirms the message by repeating what was sent.

3. The sender confirms this is correct. If not, the sender must resend the correct message.

Types of Communication

There are three ways we communicate:

Written: emails, letters, documents

Verbal: telephone, video calls

Face to face: meetings, conversations in person

The majority of our time spent communicating with others in business is through the written form. It is easy to write or respond to an email or prepare a document, as these tasks can be carried out to suit our own schedule. Yet, there are more issues with written communication, as the words we use can be interpreted differently by different people.

Our language and culture can also influence how we write and what it means. For example, certain words in sentences can sometimes be interpreted as the opposite of what we actually mean. Long written messages are more likely to be confusing. The shorter the message, the less likely mistakes are to be made. Keep it short, simple and to the point.

Verbal communication is preferred by many in business, as the message can be expressed with feelings, conveyed by the sender or receiver's tone of voice. It is more effective to communicate a message with feelings as it can make the receiver more receptive. Immediate responses from the receiver confirm how a message has been received and allow the sender to respond or acknowledge immediately. A one-to-one phone call can be easily arranged, but a group phone or video call often requires pre-planning, as it needs to fit with everyone's diary.

The most effective form of communication is meeting face-to-face, either on a one-to-one basis or with a group. In meetings, body language comes into play. It is not just what you say, it is how you say it and how your body conveys the message. The message is heard, seen and received loud and clear. In face-to-face meetings, the receiver's responses are more direct and convey to the sender whether the message has been received and understood.

Communication Styles

Understanding ourselves and others is a basic, essential skill for effective communication. We all have different ways of processing information. We all have a primary and secondary style of communication.

Shirlaws' TFK framework illustrates the different processes of the individual in understanding ourselves and others, and how best to communicate with each other. It is a framework explaining the Thinking, Feeling and Knowing communication styles:

T Thinking-style people use their brains to process words, data and information. Strong thinkers are analytical and take time to get all the facts straight before making a decision.

F Feeling-style people use their body to connect with others. They are attracted to visuals, pictures and colours in their communications with others. Strong feelers make decisions based on how they feel in consultation with others.

K Knowing-style people use their knowledge and experiences to communicate with others. Strong knowers make decisions quickly and communicate in a short, direct manner.

Awareness of our own and others' communication styles will allow the use of different ways to connect with others, making communication more effective. As businesses are likely to have a mix of thinkers, feelers and knowers, the outcome will be a greater awareness of others and how we work together, sharing a common language in understanding and connecting with each other.

A simple observation of individual communication styles can be seen at a group dining event:

> The thinker will take their time to read through the whole menu and assess the combination and choice of the starters, mains and desserts.

> The feeler will ask others for their opinion and take time to decide how they feel and what they want. Their decision will be influenced by others.

> The knower will glance through the menu briefly and select their dinner based on what they want, possibly before they sit down. They are often frustrated with others who take time to decide what they want.

Team Profiles

Effective communication by the senior management team and other teams across a business is fundamental to its success and growth. Profiling a team will allow the individual to communicate differently with each team member. The outcome will be a business that is fun to work in, creating and sharing new ideas and making quick decisions to move the business forward, thus generating growth.

An observation of a board of directors' profiles shows:

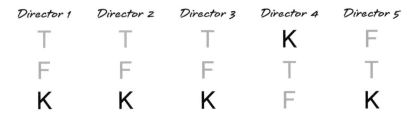

This business is dominated by strong thinkers. They communicate well with each other and they make decisions after processing all the information prepared. At board meetings, there is a lot of discussion and the decision-making process is thorough and slow. As expected, the business is overwhelmed with a lot of data and discussion based on content. Often, the board will delay making a decision on a major issue and request for further research and documentation.

The strong feeler on the board is aware of, and understands, the profiles of his fellow directors. He communicates well with them by applying his thinking communication style.

The strong knower in the business is often frustrated that the board takes too long to make decisions. However, he also communicates well with his fellow directors by applying his thinking communication style.

To find out your individual profile, go to:
www.shirlawscompass.com/tfk

CHAPTER 12

Valuation

Questions often asked:

> What is my business worth?
>
> When do I need to value the business?
>
> How do I create a high value for my business before I exit?

Every business has a value of what it is worth to the owners or others, inside or outside the business. The value of a business is time dependent, now or sometime in the future. It is easier to establish the value of a business now, than sometime in the future, as there will be unpredictable factors that affect valuation.

The question of valuation is raised in a business when:

> Business owners wish to exit and sell the business.
>
> A third party wishes to buy the business.
>
> The management team wish to buy the business.

Many owners of businesses are happy working in the business and are not concerned with the value until they wish or need to exit due to retirement, poor health or personal reasons. Sometimes, owners who have been working in the business for a long period of time may also wish to leave immediately due to stress – *'I've had enough, and I want to get out now'*. In the case of a quick exit, the value of the business is known as a 'fire sale', where the value may not be maximised.

Owners can often plan ahead for their exit from their business and the valuation forms part of their exit strategy.

Exit Strategy = Succession Plan + Business Valuation

Valuation Strategy

To maximise the value, a business needs a right vision, a right strategy and a right structure:

Maximum	=	Right	+	Right	+	Right
Valuation		Vision		Strategy		Structure

A **right vision** in a business is the definition of where the business wants to be and why.

A **right strategy** is the plan that the business is implementing to achieve its vision.

A **right structure** is the relationship between everyone in the business to facilitate the right responsibilities, reporting and communication.

When a business creates plans and implements its vision, strategy and structure, it confirms that the business's operations are functional, the revenue is growing, and they know what the future looks like.

Valuation Model

There is a range of valuation formulas for calculating the value of a business in the marketplace. The basic model for the valuation of a business is defined as:

Valuation = Profit x Multiple (V = P x M)

The profit of a business is the turnover minus the expenditure. The average profit in a business is the average of the last three years of accounted profits, with different weightings for each year.

Most owners understand profits and will naturally work towards maximising profits over a three-year period before departure. This is carried out in three areas:

1. Increase revenue by selling more.
2. Decrease costs by improving staff efficiency and reducing expenditure.
3. A combination of both.

Every industry has a multiple—an industry norm, a benchmark—with which to compare one business to another. There will be some businesses that achieve higher multiples than others, depending on many factors.

A business can improve its multiple by increasing its assets.

AssayCS (**www.assaycs.com**) explains that there are seven layers of valuation where the multiple can be increased:

Layers 1 and 2 relate to the operations of the business. When a business has established these, the multiple will increase from the industry benchmark of 1 to 1.2 times.

Layers 3, 4 and 5 relate to revenue. When a business has defined its core products, product extensions and new products, as well as referrals and sales strategy, the multiple will increase to 1.5 times.

Layers 6 and 7 relate to the strategy on positioning and scale. The multiple will increase to 4 times.

V+7	Scale	4.0
V+6	Positioning + Brand	2.0
V+5	Distribution	1.5
V+4	New Products	1.4
V+3	Product + Product Extensions	1.3
V+2	System + Infrastructure	1.2
V+1	Talent + Culture	1.1
V	Industry Benchmark	1.0

See an example below of a valuation prepared for a small professional business, where the owner wanted to exit and sell the business:

	YEAR 1	YEAR 2	YEAR 3	AVERAGE
Turnover	£465k	£390k	£434k	£430k
Expenditure	£280k	£300k	£334k	£306k
Profit	£84k	£48k	£44k	£57k

Information extracted from the past three years' accounts shows:

The turnover is quite consistent.

The expenditure is increasing.

The business is profitable, although profit is declining.

Average profit over the past three years is £57,000.

The industry benchmark multiple for a professional business is 4.5.

From the valuation model, the business is in layer V+5, creating a multiple of 1.5 times the industry benchmark:

$V = P \times M$

$= £57,000 \times 4.5 \times 1.5$

$= £384,750$

The owner sold and exited from his business within three months.

Recommended Reading List

Built to Last by James Collins and Jerry Porras

Connect Through Think Feel Know by Clive Hyland

Delivering Happiness by Tony Hsieh

Effective Coaching by Myles Downey

Find Your Why by Simon Sinek, David Mead and Peter Docker

Good to Great by James Collins

Ikigai: The Japanese Secret to a Long and Happy Life by Héctor García and Francesc Miralles

More Money, More Time, Less Stress by John Rosling

Natural Born Winners by Robin Sieger

Start With Why by Simon Sinek

Trillion Dollar Coach by Eric Schmidt, Jonathan Rosenberg and Alan Eagle

You Can Heal Your Life by Louise Hay

Acknowledgements

"Coaching is about asking a lot of challenging questions and letting the person come up with the answers."

Darren Shirlaw

Many people in both my business life and personal life have contributed towards my ability to write this book, knowingly or otherwise. In business, these are my clients, fellow coaches, mentors and trainers who have supported me in my coaching journey over the past 15 years.

Thank you to all my clients for inviting me into your businesses, giving me the opportunity to coach you, and be with you on your business journey.

Specific thanks to:

Alan Anthony, Managing Director, Threesixty Architecture

David Page, Founding Partner, Page\Park

Duncan McLean, Managing Director, IPIG

Joanna Dunbar, Managing Director, UK Health Enterprises

Ken Ross, CEO, RDR Ltd

Lynsay Bell Manson, Managing Director, LBA Architecture

Richard Neilson, Managing Director, Quantum Solutions

Stephen McGhee, Managing Director, LMA

Steven Denham, Managing Director, Denham/Benn

To my former fellow coaches and trainers at Shirlaws, thank you for introducing me to the art of coaching and teaching me the context and content of business coaching. This was a life-changing experience and allowed me to see the business world in a completely different light. Specific thanks to Darren Shirlaw, Ian Shirlaw, Rosslyn Tasker and Lorne Patten.

My thanks to Ben Brodie at Threesixty Architecture for preparing all the graphics and diagrams.

About Robin Th'ng

"The goal is not to be better than the other man, but your previous self."

Dalai Lama

Robin Th'ng was born in Miri, Malaysia, and lived in Brunei in his early childhood.

He won a scholarship to study architecture at the Robert Gordon Institute of Technology, Aberdeen, and later transferred to, and graduated from, the University of Strathclyde. He was awarded a research fellowship with ABACUS, where he pioneered and developed architectural software for applications in business.

Robin joined a small architect private practice in Scotland and progressed to become a managing partner. During his 23-year tenure, the business grew to become one of the most successful architect practices in the UK.

He then joined Shirlaws, an international coaching business in the UK, for 10 years. During that period, he grew the coaching business in Scotland and gained a wide range of experience working with SME and corporate businesses.

Robin is the Founder of iTHNG, which specialises in providing business and executive coaching for professional businesses in the construction industry.

He is happily married to May and has four children, Pollyanna, Robbie, Nikki and Natalie and three grandchildren, Jack, Max and Cassian.